TABLES

TABLES

Poems by

ALFRED CORN

Press 53
Winston-Salem

Press 53, LLC
PO Box 30314
Winston-Salem, NC 27130

First Edition

SILVER CONCHO POETRY SERIES

Cover design by Kevin Morgan Watson

Cover art, "Boy Seated at Table with Red-Checkered Cloth (1960),"
by Fairfield Porter, used by permission of Parrish Art Museum,
Southampton, New York.

Author photo by Leslie McGrath

Printed on acid-free paper
ISBN 978-1-935708-74-2

To Clement Ruggeri,
kind and generous friend

"…they're fighting that I
may yet recover from the disease, My
Self; some have it lightly; some will die."

—Marianne Moore, "In Distrust of Merits"

"History, Stephen said, is a nightmare from which
   I am trying to awake."

—James Joyce, *Ulysses*

"Misce stultitiam consilis brevem:
   Dulce est desipere in loco."

(Intersperse your sage teachings with an occasional joke.
   It's pleasing to be harebrained at times.)

—Horace, *Odes*, Book Four, xii

ACKNOWLEDGMENTS

Artful Dodge "Braggioni," "After Valéry"

AWP Chronicle, "New England/China"

Barrow Street, "Connectedness of All Things," "Letter to Grace Schulman"

Bloom, "Chestnuts Roasting"

Chattahoochee Review, "Upbringing"

Commonweal, "Coals"

Connotation Press, "Letter to Robert Pinsky"

Cutthroat, "Vines," "What the Thunder Says"

Electronic Poetry Review, "Solvents"

Hika, "Snow Bagatelle"

The Hudson Review, "Priority," "CORN, ALFRED D., JR.   34833361 T44 450"

Image, "St. Anthony in the Desert"

The James White Review, "Series Finale"

Literary Imagination, "Nemo," "The Front Line"

The Long Poem (UK), "New England/China"

Magma (UK), "The Front Line," "Lighthouse"

The Melic Review, "La Luz Azul/The Blue Light"

Nebraska Review, "Domus Caerulea"

The Nation, "From the Prompter's Box," "Fùtbol"

The New England Review, "Poem Found in *Two Years Before the Mast*"

The New York Sun, "CORN, ALFRED D. , JR.   34833361 T44 450"

Nimrod, "After Cocteau"

nth position, "Solvents"

Open City, "Ultra"

PN Review, "Domus Caerulea," "Hadrian," "Hereford"

Poetry London (UK), "Audubon," "Alf Laylah Wa Laylah," "Fig"

Poetry Review (UK), "Fùtbol," "Horizontal"

Prairie Schooner, "Oklahoma"

Shenandoah, "Resources"

Slate, "Dinner Theater," "In-Flight Couplets Composed During a Bomb Alert" and "Window on the World"

Valparaiso Poetry Review, "Bond Street Station Underground"

Washington Square, "Letter to Marilyn Hacker"

The Wolf, "Bond Street Station Underground"

Anthologies

"After Cocteau" (under the title "Young Girl Sleeping") appeared in *The Yale Anthology of French Poetry* (2005), edited by Mary Ann Caws. "Connectedness of All Things" was reprinted in the anthology *Babylon Burning: 9/11 Five Years On* (2007), edited by Todd Swift. "Solvents" was recorded for an anthology CD titled *Lifelines* 2, edited by Todd Swift to benefit Oxfam.

TABLES

TABLES

HORIZONTAL

Gray light stone light light of the middle ages
merged with the western rain
it softens curtain panels to a blank
canvas I silhouette
a hand against four fingers veed
open thumb elled
aside opposable but not opposed
it won't not here next to
you untangle a place or time
or hold anything down
I mean when spoons match up as well as ours

WHAT THE THUNDER SAYS

A crack a second and a third splinter as the dam fractures
Soundbolts spiking down through granite a dynamite
That means concussive rage detonations battering
Skull ribcage spine an earthquake high in the ramparts
Stone ramparts blocking a sun now too shell-shocked to rise

The houses implode roof skewed off to one side a broken
Beam crushes doors windows in its crazed veer a drill
Hurled into rooms to shiver walls timbers floor ratcheting
Through the garden spewing floods of dirt flagstones spun
Into the air while a tank dropped from the clouds flattens on impact

Whole quarries of rock shear off tumble smash wreck their way
Off the mountain megatons of shattered booms packed stacked
On the air collapsing around your ears and what the din sounds
Out is the last thought which already owns you you and yours
Nothing holds off the thunderstone I am it says your death.

RESOURCES

Late May remakes the park, even
the part laid out behind wrought iron
fence railings, one pigeon on promenade,
crisp feathers a not so common
cocoa and dishrag-gray, the compact head
ticking along fast forward,
a changing silk rainbow as its collar.
Heavy leafage, pollen and nectar poured
from the locust flowers' galactic cloud...
Breathe in the fragrant troposphere, then pause:
and let today recover its first cause.

                    *

I've been paging through compendia and sources
to find that timeless tale, the one in which
a peasant princess wearing star-bright pearls
(the dowry offered by a guardian witch)
drops her gaze and lets a sneering rival
snatch away the favor. Who, when she forces
its clasp shut, shrieks to see her pillage shrivel
into a snarl, a torque of snakes and lizards—
the same for all wearers but the fair and gentle.

                    *

A fifties living room. "Consider the *source*."
For emphasis, her last word's octave leap
struck a dulcimer that rang out silver
as wires glinting in permanent elderly
waves, waves a tearful grandson shouldn't muss.

Consolation was built on fortitude.
Dunces spat venom, ragged us with their cheap
jokes, but disgrace was theirs alone, the fruit
of a defective character bedeviled
by our brain's reptilian taproot. "It's misplaced

response to hurts they've undergone themselves.
Treat them as *you* should treat them, not as they
do you. Wherever we are known as ourselves,
there's love enough. Say, curly head, who made us?
Then raise your eyes, lamb, and consider the Source."

＊

Pre-summer anti-twilight lingers late,
the last knife, plate and cup not put away
till well beyond eleven. What's made me
burn insomnia's glaring kilowatt,

stacking chips on the actuarial table?
A decade's grace; then sky-high interest on the Debt....
Life-lender, you've let it stay outstanding yet
collection agencies all know my name.

Lamplight. A cloudburst of bygones. One free
hand sprawled on facing pages of a book.
"Call in thy death's head there; tie up thy fears."
Smithy of resource, the ringing anvil shapes
what sleep's lithe silver ouroboros took
from one day's solo round, till the prologue clears:

*Late May remakes the park, even
the part laid out behind wrought iron
fence railings, one pigeon on promenade...*

＊

DINNER THEATER

Characters treading not quite level pine
Boards number, first off, Carafe, sweating beads
Of coolant on her Delft-blue leaves and birds.
Then enter Sirloin, crusty, rare, supine,

Giving his aromatic agony
Away in pink tears drained into the dark
Platter's symmetrically branching tree.
Sharp Knife starts bantering with Mrs. Fork—

Quips and metallic whispers re Parsnip,
The fossil he's been trying to butter up.
Pepper's gambits are pungent, but poor Salt
Gets maudlin as the meal grinds to a halt.

And now the attentive, worn-out Napkins, who move
Toward lips whose service, too, resembles love.

CHESTNUTS ROASTING

1960-1970

A turn a sigh I'd pull into the driveway

At supper the bibled iron of his voice
Joshing its way into some slantwise judgment

Candles never lit save in December
Starring her eyes with double pilot lights

The desserts of childhood fruitcake lemon pie
A coconut and orange salad called ambrosia

Eternal life by angels heralded by ringing jingles
Rudolf meanwhile blackballed from all reindeer

Games why because he had this scarlet nose

Series Finale

Consensus rated all my ex's, each
in his own way, "attractive," as much a comment
on character as visual appeal.
But any hour *you* walked the New York streets—
open-air runways never understocked
with star-quality icons—a new hopeful
spun on his heels to take a second look.

*

Fantasy: since percentages suggested
mine wouldn't strike, not in this incarnation,
that first bright noon expected nothing like
the voltage that jumped between reciprocals
when we stood up and pushed armchairs away
from a table littered with what was left of lunch.
Sofa accommodating our two weights,
without the routine preamble you climbed
onto my lap, shucked off your thin pink shirt,
laughing, rocking, basking in the shock,
my hand on your chest jolted by its solid
resilience and fine pelt to a reverent tremor.
Heaven, who knew, flings wide its gates like heatstroke,
and the awed extoller's bodied-forth devotion
knows no shame, it truly can't distinguish
graphic from hagiographic images.

*

Being lucky several times in love
is imperfect luck; but love it was and therefore
deserved a vow of non-comparison.
Single now, it comes to me the years
spent with you clocked in at roughly two:
the shortest of all, no epic,
a lyric, the runt of the litter.
Given we've been apart for just as long,
should I expect a spurt of adrenaline
when the search engine starts to exhume our couple
from digs where we've been dozing underground?
Well, extra innings build the strongest charge—
all the more now that it seems I've passed
the age of consent. Happy scrimmage, my last,
oh, to exhale *I love you* just once more!

*

Developing your own fiction you viewed
yourself linked with not just one more admirer
or even "life-companion" but a *writer*—
first of my soul-mates (and this includes the prof)
to whom the collected fireworks much mattered.
Sure, the praise-addicted self was flattered
by your special excellence in that regard,
the irony, I couldn't find a fable
extravagant enough to tell our story.
A documentary would have left you cold,
I mean, one featuring childhood hard knocks
you've overcome but don't like hearing mentioned;
and the same goes for seropositive status.
None of that explained your inner you,
the fan of classic movies, staunch disciple
of Woolf, Balzac, Van Gogh, and the Bauhaus.

*

I know, this portrait, this portfolio
will strike you as a negative, worked up
to dodge description as a solipsist
whose exaltation tends to erase its object.
But won't your next short story right the balance?
We always loved like fencers, darts and touchés
red as those paradoxical valentines
both of us sported just above the heartbeat.

*

Enough. Or nearly: considering that at least
the text might score, I'm adding a finale
that deals with exits, endings as such, the brief
cinematic romance winding down, replaced
with midnight skies and comprehensive stillness.
A cypress, distant rooftops, moonstruck howls,
and, above, a black screen exiled energies
prick out in complex patterns. Light once seen
never returns except as mind returns
to it; yet old magnetic flames—Arcturus,
Sirius, Aldebaran, Polaris—
will be recycling their canonic fables,
new only as the upturned eye is new,
each starlit gazer offering those classics
the renovating favor of hushed attention.

ULTRA

One sluggish lightning bolt
of tar, its jags and slashes
betraying an affinity

with barbed wire—where else but out there
in the open field? Frazzled
actor ratcheted into the foreground,

your slipshod chuckle punched up the role,
and when you could mimic a greased
colluder you did. As a favor

just for tonight will you slide the rheostat
down a few notches, declaw the last radon
star, climb up and slap a patch on that roving

socket? Look: one skydiver's
out of restraints already, spread-eagled rag doll
cartwheeling the vault, locked in an eddy

until snagged, dragged, on the first spar of daybreak.

Window on the World

Time after time a glitch immobilized the screen
At *Windows Is Shutting Down*, the program icon hanging

Fire in paradoxical support of its sign-off
Caption during that long month of graveyard shifts

And pre-dawn vigils I spent sifting online fallout
Of terror, pity, and insight posted to the globe.

Nine-Eleven, Nine-Eleven, hear it, a ravaged
SOS, our call to arms and talisman,

The dateline turning septic with its subtext, spun
Out by the Web's ten thousand orb-weavers, so many

Forwarding Auden's "Those to whom evil is done
Do evil in return." And done again by enraged

Coevals, sheer reaction's critical mass redoubling
Topical fission, escalation, devolution,

A huge acridity that spikes air-quality graphs,
That floats down on a waterproofed black jacket's yellow

And gray stripes as the bearded fireman doffs his helmet
At the sky, twin tear-streaks guttering a mask of ashes.

* *

Time travel: From our early-70s Grand Street loft space
In pre-consumer-heaven SoHo, W.

And I had watched and clocked the towers' floor by floor
Ascent, a postwar symbol of extra-military

Triumph, material and pop culture scoring where
Napalm, exfoliants and M-16s had failed.

So empire might not seem passé, tired Unity bowed
And underwrote a new production, Concept Two,

The male North Tower boasting its TV broadcast mast,
The female South, an observation deck for tourists.

A few floors down, designer restaurant, entitled
Windows on the World: Where better celebrate

The publication of a poet's debut volume?
One, we liked back then to patronize posh venues;

Two, a comment on its blue and orange jacket
Had called the book "a new window onto the world."

Consolation for not being rated the latest star—
A Seidman, Burkhard, Jordan, Piercy, or Blackburn—

It mostly worked, though befriending envy sometimes hissed,
Those years I spent cooling my heels outside fame's shortlist.

But not that day. From our table on floor 107,
I heard the City launch its anthem, steep windows framing

Brooklyn and Verazzano Bridges, the Woolworth Building,
Five high-rise mirrored boxes, Liberty, and the Harbor.

On top of the world, bask, green bardlet, in those spacious
Skies, don't aim your telephoto lens at the future.

* *

Where you'd see you, weathered, silvered, skipping farewell
Glances at a town three decades your home base.

For fame, whatever else it's not or doesn't do,
At least pays bills, the scrape and cramp that youth can finesse

Costing the veteran pain, angst, and sleeplessness.
Advanced degrees in urbanity packed up, July

2001, I dropped the gear in Drive and launched out
On the road, no landfall planned before late August.

* *

Those not tube-addicts will understand how, absent
A shaken call from a friend reporting the first strike,

One nauseated witness fewer would have seen, no,
Felt in his gut both deathbolts and the dual collapse.

Felt through the media—TV, Net, and, before
Blackout, cell phones. Somehow I got through to friends,

None of them missing but all choked by poison gas,
Paralyzed speechless with the inconceivable.

* *

Because the dead disown inflated claims, I have to
Question several statements made about the towers:

"An architectural masterpiece." No, they were *tall*, some
High-rises elsewhere taller, and many better designed.

"The hub of U.S. geopolitics and trade."
No, few that worked there qualified as global players.

"Site of the first homeland attack since Independence."
No, see 1812, the Civil War, Pearl Harbor.

"The modern era's worst disaster." No, consider
Stalingrad, Dresden, Hiroshima, the Holocaust.

"New York's chief symbol." Not, in all honesty, to most,
No match for the Bridge, Ellis Island, or Liberty.

* *

But place detachment beside the sense of mutilation
Inferno's aftermath would trigger six weeks later

When my night flight on American approached
Ground Zero. Spotlit, twenty-four/seven rubble clearance

Replaced twin peaks naïveté once took for granted
In the downtown spreadsheet printout of Manhattan's skyline.

Pilgrimage to the site required a mask to filter
Fumes that stank of burnt synthetics and calcium.

I choked up gazing at that iconic shard, a giant
Upended metal thumb-piano keyboard whose ragged

Elegy roaring earthmovers snuffed out as they
Processed remains of two thousand and more deceased.

Who won't be back. And yet, almost as though to highlight
Absence, TV movie reruns these past months

Have been reviving, in how many slots, an image
Both stricken and eternal: standard chopper panning

Shots of the postcard skyline thrusting at us, and, lo,
The stereophonic comeback Symbol, tall as life.

* *

Mortality, box-cutter in hand, conquers all,
A cockpit-crasher, terminating our dazed pilots,

Jamming the vessel's forward mandate… Does that senior
Chef taking bread from ovens in his vintage kitchen

Lofted among the clouds, detect invisible
Omens in the autumn light?—a bass-clef hum,

Endtime launched on its unyielding slalom, twin
Convergence that will call for shutdown once our client,

The kamikaze who refused to book a table,
Shows up to firebomb celebration's ever-afters.

* *

Befriending soul, when lethal smoke begins to rush
From the broken towers' crematory, will we hang back

In burning topicality? *No*, sings the window.
Hold hands, eyes meeting as they never have before.

Today your tandem launches out on visionary
Sunlight, to cast its lot with a world without end—

One extra encore for a pair upheld in zero
Gravity, anti-Lucifers, twin morning stars,

United Symbol here that nothing puts asunder,
Love's company unlost so long as love proves life.

Coals

No two alike, exchanging nuances
Of fervor, each core permeable

To wingbeats lit with utterance's
Halation, golden streambed gravel

Immersed in a baptismal shimmer
Nearly inaudible but never stilled....

Great-grandmother's coal fires winters
Back in the scriptural forties filled

Our rooms with thick carbonic reek—
With prophesying infrareds

So fierce they stung (and sting) the cheek
That then put up with and now laments

Old age's kiss. She'd say: *Repay*
Evil with good, our sole defense.

Kindness heaps coals of fire on hatred,
Ill will.... Then bring one from the grate

For lips more drawn to blame than to amends.

CORN, ALFRED D., JR. 34833361 T44 450

Try and muster the first unshaven dogface
to call them "dog tags," sardonic smile aimed
at a pair of steel and nickel leaves die-stamped
with his name, a license to kill or be killed.

Like some legendary bullet-stopping Bible,
gemini chiming shields suspended
on a beaded chain and slung around
infantrymen's necks must from time to time
have saved their lives. When not, the medics would
at least know where to ship parts left behind.

A ball of string, the globe has spun and shrunk
since Daddy's hitch, the upshot, any conflict
within days goes worldwide. ID'd and daily fed
into databanks, what's my answer when a voice
high in the nonexistent dome overhead
asks how I view our military safeguards?

Good thing those soldiers couldn't see into
the future. Their bead-chain rosaries failed to say
what world was in the pipeline, and previews
wouldn't have much helped steel the resolve
of a man slogging on through muck and ordnance.

A pathetic booster, I have to leave him there
in his determined past, where he can do his bit
for Mother and us, the jingle dangling on his chest
spelling his name (and my name, once removed),
urging him not to let down the brand; also helpful
in case he fell, too messed up to be recognized.

From the Prompter's Box

Those first-nights when I see my charge's panic,
And, in quick whispers, slip him mislaid lines,
Untangled recognition scenes will light
A face, inflected sense revive a flagging
Voice; and my inner rating service smiles.

No. No, the program never credits Prompter.
The same as nursing, ours is a self-reliant
Calling regarded as its own reward...
Although, in fairness, the brightest stars remember
To breathe a private "thank you" at the curtain.

Just like a turntable set, sight lines shifted
The day I gazed at that smooth slab of his—
The Unknown Soldier, who then began to prompt:
Mobilized for an afterlife of marble,
I'm bunked here in a tomb not granted those

Whose shining names appear on that bronze roster.
Distinctions should be met with gratitude;
Which holds, at least until the censers exit.
I paid what we all owe. And would again,
Allowed to exchange this blank for clear inscriptions

Recording what I did beside my name.
A greater loss than death? Identity!
Homage rings hollow on an anonymous crypt.
From nil and dark the self I knew calls out
For the small tag love once attached me to.

St. Anthony in the Desert

To be filled with that hallowed emptiness
The hermit sojourns in a desert cave.
Fasting and prayer will make seclusion safe,
His daily bread, each word the Spirit says.

Chimera stirs and rears her dripping head;
A slack-skinned reptile puffs and makes a face;
Vile, harrowing nightmares shimmer through long days;
The sun beats a brass gong and will not set.

Faint shadow on cave walls, you foretell grief
Or joy, not known till whose the profile is:
Love itself may corrupt and then deceive
Its object, hiding venom in a kiss.
Anthony kneels, embraces his fierce lot,
And hears: *Be still, and know that I am God.*

ALF LAYLAH WA LAYLAH

The Book of a Thousand Nights and a Night

Sesame opens on a trove of palm-tree locales
From the Indus to the Maghreb, Baghdad, Mecca,
Damascus, Cairo, a realm where chance and waywardness
Ripple what dunes flank the snakelike silk roads,
Where Allah, may He be praised, patterns Creation,

Sending djinn, tsunamis of coiling sea serpents

Or birds broad as mountains, to punish wrongdoers
And reward the good—whose names come twinned,
Sindbad the Seaman and Sindbad the Landsman,
Or Abu Kir the Dyer and Abu Sir the Barber,
Personae spun like wool on fortune's wheel

Into narratives sprouting ancillary tales

Set in turn with cameo fables, a nested sequence
Of concentric matrices linked by one umbilical,
The hypnotic, purred gestations of Scheherazade,
Plotter of addictive, oil-lamp-lit recitatives
For a thousand nights and one, destinies imaged

So as to convert impending death into audience,

A pragmatism delirious as a carpet theorized
Along the lines of cosmogony's tautly strung
Chaos, yet weaving, too, a human precinct, a mihrab
Where prayer is texted to the Compassionate,
The All-giving, whose hands hold keys to worlds

Seen and unseen, that His mercies may not cease.

Toys in the Hospital Gift Shop

A stubby zebra with wallpaper stripes;
The hacksaw gape of a felt crocodile;
A sleek fire engine and its coiling hose;
Hand-puppet clowns with green or orange hair:

One of these should soothe our kindergarten
Convalescent, who'll let it freely range
The linen snowfield mountained by his knees
Till sleep's slow carrousel-spin times him out...

What do toys want to say, why *are* they us,
Adults still snapping up and treating children
To bits of fluff that make us laugh, a lure
For the sandman's bag of animated films?

Prophets used to call the worldly sphere
A hospital, each wounded soul its patient.
Supposing our evolving globe's a wind-up
Toy, too, designed to charm its ailing Maker,

Who names deific maladies, or heals them?
What tragicomic acts provide distraction,
Teasing away eternal tears and boredom
Till evening starts to roll in, pain subsides,

And humor's snow-plow clears the path to sleep?
Whose muffled advent also snuffs Creation—
Its toys, beforehand, voicing a rote petition:
May we recur as players in your dream.

UPBRINGING

"Yes, ma'am," "No, sir!" Parents' blandest questions
Took for granted a standard honorific
When I answered. Lazy omission of which
Triggered on the spot a sharp "Yes, *who?*"
Till ma'ams or sirs—but properly intoned—
Were reinstated in the heart and mind
Of a Southern boy who had been well brought up.

A civil tongue. And basic training, too,
In table manners, being seen and not
Heard, respect for elders and for members
Of the female sex, referred to always as *ladies*
Once they were no longer girls. (A *woman*
Was someone who cleaned, invariably black,
Who said "please" and "thank you" every chance she got.)

How a gentleman behaved was dinned in
His ears from day one, an ideal as crucial
As soldiering in the army of the saints.
Yet ladies were a holier, a frailer
Vessel, deserving, therefore, special treatment.
Her parcels, you carry. What she drops, pick up.
Open the door, and let her enter first.

Into Heaven, too, it still seems plausible.
Do we ever trash a brain washed clean so early?
"The first shall be the last, and the last, first,"
Gates of Paradox inform the hopeful
Who knocks…. I give that upbringing this much:
"Let others pass before you" didn't mean
"Just freeze, and let them push on by themselves."

PRIORITY

"Mama," I called my father's new wife, long
Before my older sisters, both still mourning
Their dark-haired, stylish, much-loved parent, did.

Never in words did Daddy convey the torment
He felt when Mother died; in fact, till forced to,
Avoided even mentioning her name.

Pictures of her he put in hiding. She—
Like all invisible ideas or persons—
Loomed, she became, what, almost legendary.

No doubt he thought he should play down bereavement
So as not to jeopardize his second marriage.
The Hitchcock film *Rebecca*, had he seen that,

The one in which a wife succumbs to fears
She matters less to her beloved than
His first? As dilemmas go, it's sort of common,

Even when just divorce has torn a husband
From one he does his damnedest not to love.
Eventually her surrogates perceive

The governance of a ghostly absence, who
Trumps all those coming after. Think what gloom
Must overtake them when awareness dawns

That they can't mend a psyche hoarding grief
Or fury as its costliest possession.
Abysmal, too, must be his own reflection,

Mixed with betrayal in the second best's
Gaze, once clear and trustful—if he sees it.
So much, then, for blind censorship, dead silence,

Inverted syntax… Our first mother's name was Grace.
Virginia, we loved your sense of fun, your kindly face.

FIRST DICTIONARY

Its frontispiece a grizzled Noah Webster
In fresh-tied neck-cloth, gazing calmly westward.

Thirteenth birthday present for a searcher-
Out of meanings, who grasped that reasoned nurture

Had landscaped lexic woodlands to a plain
Instructive playing field where scrubs could train.

Also, it featured small line-drawings, four
Or maybe five per page: the human ear

In cross section; a rhesus monkey rather
Resembling the mild lexicographer

Who'd pegged him as a primate, hence our dumb
Cousin. Cuts for the alphabetic thumb

Index were sills that staggered down to a cave
Or hatch that opened for explorers brave

Enough to dive to *zero* or soar to *zenith*.
M turned up *masturbation*, synonymed with

"Self-pollution." Pollute? What for? Who would?
But yearnings named under **H**, I understood.

Alum of the OED and *American
Heritage*, can I resurrect those teen

Cardings of the word-hoard's fibrous strands,
Sonic heirloom for today's string bands

That wire and text their lyric warp and woof
On *Explorer*'s Worldwide Web? Here's partial proof

That bedside ark, no tub or leaky dud,
Offered warm shelter in the mounting flood,

Where Noah housed his couples, aardvark, zebu,
And—I think unpolluted—my kind, too.

VINES

Leanings, lavings, lashings that in cool
weather shoot forward fast as the short
clock hand and, in hot, the long.

Rockface daredevils, adjectives, rapunzels,
strategists, they reel out
a flexible antenna to get a purchase
on any scaffold or trellis in range, a grab-on,
a braiding, that sun, rain, and years will strengthen
as the minute
digital pads
cling to whatever handhold stays.

Without support, disabled, they'd flail
and collapse but, supplied by their IV's,
have the strength to dangle out clusters of flowers
or fruit, spiced wines to inhale or drink down.
Morning glory's deep Marian blue,
the dull gold stalactites of muscadet
suspended in a fume of honey,
and the climbing roses, the roses!

Against brick or stone an exact progress
is recorded, the pattern's asymmetrical
perfection tendril
by rambler inscribed and revealed
when leaves drop away:
an organic etching, grillwork balustrade,
knotted tapestry of appositives,
the saga of a dependence that kept its freedom
to be what they becomingly are.

And yet a few, like kudzu
or strangler fig, have unrestraint
twined into their very nature, they annex
all they can, imperial as wildfire,
climbers that invade, engulf, choke, ravage,
siphoning up water and blocking light
until the naïve host's swathed in deadly feathery
boas of foliage. Not satisfied, the vines tighten
to constrict the trapped trunk and branches,
and, woe, tighter still, winding, screwing, wrenching,
as the rack grows tougher,
teak or oak at last throttled sapless, foreclosed.

Yet when support though dead remains intact,
they enjoy a long-term lease of aftermath,
in preening leisure on their lofty hat-rack, king
of the mountain, rolling in the clover of themselves.
That no triumph endures they forget, we all do.
But then, at length, the work of woodworm, beetle, and dry rot
done, down tips the ghost-tree, along with its thick
invader cables, dragged to the floundering earth, snapped
off at the root, prone on the ground,
their highflown sunlit terrace forfeit.
Twilight in Valhalla. The hanging gardens have fallen,
fallen, seeds scattered to the eight winds....

These were (and will be) the Vines.

LETTER TO ROBERT PINSKY

Robert, your warm surprise reflected mine
When we met last month here in Oklahoma
After four or five years of e-mail only.
My teaching gig, your reading date: sheer chance,
Which governs half of what turns out to happen,
Can feel in retrospect like Destiny—
An antique concept unavoidable
If we maintain that Character outranks
Other engines spinning the threads of life.

But Cherokees... well, *several* nations marched here
A century ago might be allowed
To doubt it. Also, European Jews
Transported to Auschwitz. Or inhabitants
Of Gaza City, Tel Aviv, or Baghdad
In our day. Character is Destiny?
Not when shrapnel rips through civilian flesh.
(For which the guild of bards can provide a song
And dance to demonstrate art's consolations.)

You'll laugh, but Oklahoma's the New Jersey
Of the Southwest, not just because they both
Have oil-refineries. Compare the horses,
The Neo-Gothic universities;
The hard-wired habit of preferring truth
To prettier versions of reality;
And a penchant for collusion where elective
Government is concerned. No beach towns, though,
No Long Branch, like the one your books describe.

I recognize your childhood; things didn't look
Propitious. Not even you, back then, foresaw
That one day you'd be tapped as laureate,
Quoted by admirers in fifty states.
Now, flip back to the Seventies and see us
Introduced as having written that year's
"Best first books"—you, Maura, Tess, and I,
Invited by the Y to read and *prove* it.
Right then I knew you were a sure-fire bet.

And the bookie, it turns out, was right! The rest?
That's in the lap (you know the phrase) of the gods,
Whose offhand ways with me you've more than once
Countered. All right, I won't recap the facts.
We might have been mere rivals. *Are* long-term
Friends—a freebie I got from Destiny.
Warm sunlight here in Tulsa. Autumn leaves
Vacillating… When they do fall, gusts
Will bowl a *Figured Wheel* along Route 66.

OKLAHOMA

Okla, "people" and *humma,* "red," in Allen Wright's Choctaw cognomen
For this heartland state where the Trail of Tears ended—not for Cherokees
Only, but for all Five Civilized Nations, for Sac and Fox, Osage,
Muscogee and Modoc, converging on Indian Territory
Just as the Red River, the Cimarron, the Washita at length all
Resign their names to the Father of Waters... Founding Tulsey Town, Creeks
Smoked a pipe for their "Council Oak," which survived until struck by lightning,
Its successor sending roots each year closer to the Arkansas. Good
Divider, that, whether dry or flowing between well-heeled neighborhoods
And refineries transmuting black gold into half-timbered mansions
Or a sunny Italian palazzo where the foreign transplant views,
And may identify with, Tanzio's *St. John in the Wilderness.*

In Bartlesville the copper flanges of Price Tower deflect blinding
Summers that till then discouraged highrise construction in pre-A/C
Oklahoma. Frank Lloyd Wright's Atomic Age concept evidences
The need for pipelines when liquid commodities fill up new brand names
Like Phillips and Getty. Wealth would trickle down, too, to Art Deco Tulsa,
And to Greenwood's blacktown, bigotry fast on its heels, with how many
Houses torched as a dramatic backdrop for lynch law and its strange fruit.
Don't worry, someone would develop White City, but somebody else
Would make tracks as a singer of swing, the "Oklahoma Nightingale,"
Burning up the road to Kansas City in an oil-black Packard, then
Back down to OKC to gig with the Blue Devils in a Deep Deuce
Café where elusive brilliance, beguiling the midnight hour over
A scarred deal table, tapped its toe and took notes for *Invisible Man.*

The mapped outline is a schematic hand or gun, with the Panhandle's
Index or barrel drawing a bead on former Comanche grasslands.
Stolid one-horse towns like Guymon, Beaver, and Texhoma endure that
Measureless vacancy, its natural monument the Black Mesa,
Noted as the highest elevation and a landmark transition
To the True West. Peculiar how four geographic sectors converge
On one pivotal state, the pipeline crossroads for an automotive
Nation. When Kerouac got his kicks on Route 66, he may have
Led Tulsans Joe Brainard and Larry Clark to pull up stakes for the East
And become fixtures in New York's downtown arts scene, never mind the fact
That *I Remember*'s largely unread in the town remembered in it.

Daily you'll hear Westminster chimes on the campus of T.U., ringing
"Here in OK—we speak English." And so one does all over the state,
But spiked with Soonerisms, as in, "Hit's rainin big," or "The man was
Drunker than Cooter Brown," or, "I've seen goat-ropins and worm-wrestles, but
Nothing like this,"or "He looked like trouble going somewhere to happen."
Which no one said about Karen Silkwood, the night she left a union
Meeting in Crescent, invaded by plutonium, the ingested
Downer an autopsy detected, to date, not yet accounted for.

Lawton's Fort Sill, Tulsa's Lockheed, and McAlester's ammunition
Plants evidence the martial character of a people whose staked claims
Were often guaranteed by gunfire, and whose blood paid for conflicting
Rebel and Yankee loyalties. No better training for war than team
Spirit—just ask Jim Thorpe, or, since you can't, inspect the medals displayed
In his house at Yale. Where's the Wrestling Hall of Fame but in Stillwater?
Alumnus Garth Brooks could show it to you some Homecoming Weekend, just
Before the annual dustup between Cowpokes and Sooners. Notice,
On the other hand, Egypto-Great Plains grandeur as evoked by grain
Elevators towering over Elk City and Ardmore. For, when
Oklahomans weren't fighting, they were farming vast tablelands whose
Waving wheat inspired Prairie School lyrics by Rodgers and Hammerstein,
Even if "the wind comes sweeping down the plain" rather understated
Those middle counties' weather-breeding propensities. Watch the twister
As pure turmoil lowers a drill-pipe to strike a gusher of red earth
From drought-struck, depressed homesteads, a bowl that, back in 1935,
Yielded no crop to its dazed tillers but exile and the grapes of wrath.

Given that Tom Mix once mixed drinks at Guthrie's Blue Bell Bar, it makes sense
That grade-schooler John Berryman would cheer silent, horse-opera shootouts
At a Broadway movie house in Anadarko. What other sights would
A boy dream, climbing the Jacob's ladder of an oil rig out from town?
As yet there was no Indian Hall of Fame, no series of bronze busts
Cast as uncorrodable heroes: Sacajawea, Sequoyah,
Osceola, Chief Joseph, and Will Rogers. When the latter spun his
Lariat and his wry yarns, with a redeemer-like knack for liking
Every man he could wink at, populism itself paved the road to
Fame and wealth. But his voice would never chime in with the bigotry of
Zealots bowing to an idol King James commissioned in former times:
'Twasn't the Cherokee way, neighbors and friends. Meanwhile, those serenely
Historic heads dreaming away an April noonday under redbuds
And cottonwoods keep their counsel, a long vista of patinated
Commemoration neglected, mostly forgotten now, at least in
The bistros of Bricktown or among the lilacs in Utica Square.

No, today's monument jolts its pilgrims into irreversible
Contemporaneity, the Age of Terror's bereaved replacement
For the Alfred P. Murrah Federal Building. Hatred has cleared space
For a reflecting pool and a lawn dotted with vacated bronze chairs,
Proving that petrochemical fertilizer has what it takes to
Blast a daycare center, and that tears don't end just because the Trail did.
Native sons deployed in Iraq may have felt pangs of recognition
When the desert air swirled with abrasion, and ordnance bushwhacked Basra.
"Weapons of mass destruction!" and "No blood for oil!" say the clashing tags
While tanks grind forward and TVs in Tahlequah and Broken Arrow
Bless the America that Woody Guthrie called your land and my land.

Since when, though, did settlers pass up the chance, before the kick-off cannon
Fired, to get a jump on rivals? Given the groundswell hills and blackjack
Oaks, the long dawdling rivers and rich bottomland, and a firmament
Starry as the one Jacob dreamed before wrestling with his renaming
Angel, what person of feeling wouldn't try to claim a tract of this
Territory? Or new Sequoyah not invent a syllabary
To frame his speech, or playwright not care to draft a sequel to *Green Grow
The Lilacs*? Red, Adamic earth drew them on even when no one knew
It rested on priceless deposits of energy—and long before
An infantry consumed its allotment of the grapes of wrath, grumbled
A cussword, and drove into the sandstorm to become invisible.

AFTER COCTEAU

Beneath the Tree of Vision's where we'll meet.
Make sure, though, that you locate the right one.
We often mix our angels up and then get stuck
With casualties done in by a manchineel.

Oh, we know already what will be said:
Ducking out early from the ball, the revel,
Beyond the range of people's wine-soaked barbs,
Not for nothing shall we have gone to bed.

Best cook up some excuse for toddling off—
Like, say, *We've booked the night flight on Air Dream.*
That, or, *We're going to change into a Persian
Garden, so we can spy on lovers' trysts.*

Sleep's the sum total of your poetry,
Young Ms., you with your lazy, dangling arm.
Dreamland's big set piece has taken you hostage.
And other options? Yawn, you couldn't care less.

LETTER TO MARILYN HACKER

Marilyn, quick-witted author of poem-epistles, I trust you
Won't mind receiving one, drafted and sent with affectionate wishes.
Willing but hesitant, writers take up a new genre or subject,
Swearing they'll ditch it if stalled—or if soundings discredit the channel.
Didn't we say that the patron of meter's most likely Saint Rita?
Mother and guardian, vet these hexameters' dactyls and spondees!

First off, a grateful salaam for companionship during my visit.
Paris with you as accomplice was bracing and new—like the day we
Walked up to Belleville, *flâneurs* on a boulevard Walter
Benjamin's gold-rimmed bifocals must on occasion have X-rayed.
Yet, since the Twenties, worlds have collided, and strong multi-ethnic
Pressures have reshaped that neighborhood. Jews from Tunisia, Chinese,
Gallic *Français*, and Maghrebis from most of North Africa live there.
Barring a few minor set-tos, they seem to be getting along, while
Minding their shops and own business, a model of urban accord. So
Skeptics can't call you "utopian" once they assimilate Belleville's
Live affidavit that differences *don't* always turn into armed camps.

Next on the docket came Quai de Jemmapes, the Canal calmly trundling
Waters a subtle tint chemists once termed "Paris green." Leafy plane trees
Planted at one end provided a shade we abandoned for sunlight,
Opting to cross the arched bridge farther down. At the top of which we paused,
Charting the prospect like trekkers, like Aragon's *paysans de Paris*.
Just at that moment a barge on its way to the lock passed beneath us,
Marking its progress with sinewy furrows. Detritus of some sort,
Subfusc, anonymous, bobbed there, remember? An incident Henry
James once described in a letter resurfaced: How, when his friend Constance
Fenimore-Woolson had plunged to her death from a window in Venice,
He'd been recruited to help with arrangements. What fell to his lot was
Distributing all of her gowns. But, instead, he decided to "drown" them—
Where but in *Canale Grande*, the smartest expatriate address? Black
Laces and histories darkened as each was slipped overboard. Weirdly,
None of them sank, they all floated. He sat in his gondola, silent,
Stricken…
          A story that sounds like a fable, but what does it mean? Who
Knows? I don't. Meanwhile, that flotsam we noticed has washed away, vanished…
Besides, this is working-class Paris, not Venice of yesteryear. You turn,
Breathe, and suggest we push on. Future memories wait for adoption:
Take that new line of the Métro, which starts at the Madeleine, then six
Or possibly seven stops later concludes at the Bibliothèque François
Mitterrand, *i.e.*, the National Library. Proust I assume would
Smile at that—Mallarmé, too, since he said that the world was designed to
End as a book. Which makes sense if we add that a book (I mean good ones)
Will backslide, emerging as world-stuff or "life" once again. As your own do,
Marilyn—poet, American, francophone homegirl in Paris,
Recentest torchbearer in the tradition of Gertrude and Alice,
Natalie Barney, Renée Vivienne, Djuna Barnes, Janet Flanner,
Updates of *Liberty Storming the Barricades*. Sometimes the right wing
Tries to disparage a vocal progressive—which need not concern one
Whose manifest excellence writers and readers in several countries
Honor. Lutetia smiles, and her diadem sports a new brilliant.

FIG

Dessert as ravishment, the taster drunk
In, the haver having its haver, pink
Papillae jelled in flesh whose lush rose kiss
Soothes me into mouthing all Provence
Some August gravid with syruped ooze and essence.

Lapped in black-and-olive purple chamois,
Plump as Istanbul's Haghia Sophia,
Platonic figure for the "whatness" of sweet:
If I ever try to build a temple,
You, and no onion, will top off its steeple.

Groping for comparisons, a peer,
What's to put forward but that sleek green fellow,
The veiny, five-lobed leaf your wineskin swelled
Beside?—like the one Vatican marbles wear
To spare shy gazers a betraying blush.

THE FRONT LINE

Did the sand-crab's shrinking step
Ever draw and keep a sunlit profile?
If you're waiting for a sculptor,
breathing itself is what I'd try to cut.

Some graveyard-shift prophet's cursing
the back alleys, his choicest brimstone aimed
at a sprawl of lush-lifers immersed
in lukewarm media behind their shades:

Funguses, nighthawks, you
whose lungs and substance decompose
in blank rooms wrung emptier by echoes,
have you never hung up your phones,
stubbed out Camels and asked why you've clung to
shreds of a thug's flung-down arrogance?

Elsewhere and outside,
we're the fiddle tucked
under pleasure's chin, a high-wire
ensemble coaxing front-line
alchemy and catgut
standards to dialogue the project.

Audubon

Early America's gone, extinct like the passenger
Pigeon, skies once an avalanche of migration
Now vacant but for clouds and vapor trails, the rare
Vector of bleating Canada geese, or a lone mallard.
And the land below laid bare, its forests cut and burned,
Demoted to tarmac, to strip malls and gated suburbs.

When ancestors at seven removes paused to scan
The green wild, impassable except where pierced
By trails non-natives couldn't scout, they guessed
More than was sayable about the unsurveyable,
And their own intrusion trivial. Audubon differed.
Subduing the awe reconnaissance stirred in him,
He leaned on his rifle atop the sharp promontory,
And indreamed a misted river valley grown vocal
With piped solfege from the birds of America.

Brushstrokes of oil or wash won their idea.
Taut silk feathers extended a fan to grasp buffeting
Updrafts, a shot taken on the wing, one gape-staring
Fish cramponed in airborne rapture, nature's tandem
Food chain captured and shipped to the Royal Society.

What he couldn't send was context—limitless terraces
Of air, the woodlands slip-knotted with vine and briar,
Creeks rich with tannin, the crossfire gaze of bear and cougar,
Scats, a ribcage stripped clean by crook-necked scavengers,
Insurgence of mosquito tribes, ponds paved with lilies,
A singular glycerine pearl affixed to each veined disc.
Epochs that saw the uprush of aeronautic tribes
Filmed in mirroring watercolor are passed and gone.
A wilderness, a fauna, erased. Not banished, vanished.
It won't return, or not until we go. Passengers.

In-Flight Couplets Composed During a Bomb Alert

London–St. Petersburg, August 14, 2006

Mind, though they've banned material counterparts,
Your conscious page and pen got past the guards.

Think back to Mandelshtam at the Black Sea,
Composing silently, invisibly...

"It must be memorable." Yes, or else
Our uninscriptions will unwrite themselves.

Then, too, if bombs incinerate this brain,
It won't recall so much as my own name.

Exile, silence, equal oblivion?
Ask Mandelshtam. His *Tristia* may have been

The only book an author ever wrote
Each word of which the beloved got by heart.

Words fade to black if not made memories of.
Love, if it means to live, is spoken love.

NEMO

Not named, only alluded
slantwise to; unclaimed
and never credited,
however often debited.
In silence heard; inferred;
and even preferred.

Omitting's one way to have included,
but poorer than a nod, a spoken glance—
this rare, spangled, straightforward instance.

SOLVENTS

Ex-combatant, relearning human laws you'll cleanse the taint,
Your scarred or calloused hand remembering gentleness, restraint.

Whose faces are they, turned aside to avoid the blank horizon?
Shores know the river's grinding ice-floes strike without restraint.

"Man is born for trouble as the sparks fly upward." True,
But why quote Scripture if you lack the virtue of restraint?

Today's suspended sun slips down a single spider's thread.
Occasion makes the thief, and avarice will trump restraint.

Encapsulate the cosmos in a single brown fern seed?
O wildfire insight, innocent of what's meant by restraint.

Telephones, cars and travel clocks each passing year grow lighter.
But facts suggest one country failed to use them with restraint.

This morning a boy washed our windows to a brilliant tango,
Its limpid tempi attaining freedom only through restraint.

When Laura hailed the dawning Canyon, echoes proved milestones,
Not one of them recycling antique habits of restraint.

On pain of happiness, reopen that book you always loved.
To postpone ending it, you'll have to exercise restraint.

The Alfred Stagger Lee once passed his dice to tossed them west,
Pure chance a complement, no, *compliment* paid to restraint.

La Luz Azul

San Miguel de Allende
Día de la Asunción

Mediodía. Ligeros velos
Transparentes del ancho cielo….

En la estancia una sombra amorfa,
Blanda, no acababa de anunciar
Ese alto silencio que jamás
Ha de callar.

Tan comprensiva
Como dulce, recíbeme, luz
azul, que colmas los rincones…

¿Pues, inmóvil? No, mejor fuera
Salir en busca del asunto,
La palabra de mortal piedad
Caída como una flor ardiente
Entre las piedras de la calle.

THE BLUE LIGHT

San Miguel de Allende
Feast of the Assumption

Twelve noon. The open sky's transparent
Weightless veils.

In the room, a mild, amorphous
Gloom wouldn't give up announcing
That exalted silence that will never
Again hold its peace.

As comprehensive
As you are gentle, gather me in, blue
Light, you, filling up the corners...

Immobilized, then? No, better to go out
In search of the assumed subject—
The word, embodied, compassionate,
Fallen like a flame-red flower
Among the street's rough cobblestones.

Written by the author in Spanish (previous page) and translated by him into English.

BRAGGIONI

after Katherine Anne Porter

He poses on a straight-backed chair
too small for his heavy, swelling ripeness, night
after night waiting for Laura
in the upper room of her house.
Though tired of her hairpins, her tight
sleeves, again she'll have to listen
to the furry, mournful voice
of her employer, the revolutionist.
If she could undress, pull a nightgown
over her head, lie down and sink
into sleep… But Braggioni's *moved*, he wants to sing.

Lupe will bring a plate of rice,
a cup of chocolate. But "Chocolate
thickens the voice,"
he says and takes nothing.
Perhaps because of his Tuscan
peasant father, his patrician Mayan mother,
he can almost forgive
Laura for being a *gringuita*—
thin, but with large breasts
her dark blue serge dress fails
to conceal. A white collar
edged not with machine-made lace,
no, with a delicate cobweb
fluted by someone's fine needle—
a frilled comment
on tormented idealism,
a prop for everywoman's nun-like stoicism.

On her lap, a cloth-bound book lies open,
the printed page's rigid consolation
almost erasing what he says, sings, does.
She must resist without appearing to
resist his kinky yellow hair, his yellow shoes,
his yellow hanky redolent of Jockey
Club; his lyrics, passionately off-key;
his specialized insolence.
A cureless wound of self-esteem
like Braggioni's demands precise attention...
Meanwhile, she does what can be done for prisoners,
bringing news, invented assurance, whichever
narcotics the men prefer to help them dream.
Borrowing money from the Roumanian agitator,
she gives it to his enemy, the Polish agitator.
Mornings in Xochimilco she teaches her small, shy
charges, who bring roses and marigolds to decorate
"ticher's" desk. Brown faces alight,
giggling opportunists; and she is their jailor.

Braggioni suggests it, therefore she oils and loads
his pistols. "Finally, though, I pin
my faith on dynamite." In the street below
houses lean together like conspirators
under a single mottled lamp. From the garden, scent,
and the thick flowers of the jacaranda
look mauve under a layer of moonlit gauze.
His lachrymose voice
keeps cueing rounded hands that clutch or scrape
the frets... Oh, to give him a backhanded slap,
wiping that suety smile from his face!
But she hears him out, lets him appraise
her gray eyes and puzzled eyebrows,
the little cornflower-blue folder of music
and drawings, placid on a footstool.
He needs to know Eugenio took them all,
(the pills she'd brought) and then refused a doctor.
No one else must report they've found his body.
It will be Laura's task to watch this leader,
who has taught them all to sweat, invoke his mystic
power to shrug aside the death of a fool.

From the exposed nerves of the guitar
purple music and from the garden
plinking flowers join in a common arc
propelled toward the moon. "One woman
is really as good as another in the dark.
I prefer them all." Tonight, after a month's abstention
inflicted as a lesson, Braggioni returns
to his cheated wife—who will beg for pardon,
and wash his feet while her long, gray-threaded hair
spills into the basin, a pair of yellow shoes airing
beside it. Moved by this penitent,
Braggioni will weep and confer absolution.
In Laura's dream Eugenio
gets her name wrong, it sounds like "Murderer."
Her customary stance (the negation
of all external events as they occur) this time will falter.
If she would only take his hand, he might lead her to
another country. Yes, and she has guessed which one
it was. How? Because his hand is fleshless,
no more than a sheaf, a cluster
of white, petrified branches.
"Eat these flowers, little prisoner."
Purple flowers bleeding still more flowers…
If she agrees to take and eat the reason is they stanch
all hunger and all thirst.
Murderer… Murderer…

Eyes springing open, nightgown chilled and soaked,
she senses that bulk in its imaginable gloom—
Braggioni asleep, his wife's hair tangled over the bolster.
And how long will Eugenio hold out? Although
he still waits there under the jacaranda,
she gasps and chokes, does not move to the window.
Instead a bright, hard shaft of scrutiny
angles through it and photographs her room,
its task to document whatever random
evidence the dead may urge they need.

BRODSKY AT THE CAFFÉ DANTE

A Village den, not far from Morton Street,
Where you'd hosted a party just the week
Before, your birthday cake a replica
Of *A Part of Speech*'s jacket. A practical
Joke? It wasn't your most recent book,
Which blunt reviews had sort of trounced. But luck
'S a weathervane, and that year mine, too, had
Gone south, or sour, as I could tell you'd heard.

Strange: your large-scale forehead (the temple sported
A windswept curl Romantically borrowed
From Pushkin or Chateaubriand) was unlined,
Free of the trenches that gulags make or, exile.
Instead, it beamed a dynamic melancholy
Over our topics—none of them dire, really.
Ovid more vulnerable than Mandelshtam;
What Byron felt when he saw Dante's tomb.

I asked if you linked the San Marco Lion
To the address on St. Marks Place, where Auden
Had lived for decades. Just to hear his name
Unpacked a smile… In fact, the piece of cake
They'd cut you featured the King of Cats' brown sugar
Wing. Piston thrusts from that small figure,
Were counterparts to espressos we would drink—
Its caffeine still buzzing, I like to think.

AFTER VALÉRY

What smoldering secrets do youth and beauty keep,
Soul inhaling flowers through a silk mask?
From what light fare does innate ardor ask
Fuel for the radiance of a woman's sleep?

Sighs, dreams, silence; becalmed invincibly,
Peace more prevailed here than if she had wept,
Nor could swelling billows while she slept
Better protect so mild an enemy.

Sleeper, massed gold and shadowed indolence,
Tranquil abandon its own best defense,
Doe, forever couched near mounds of grapes,

If the soul is absent, summoned to Hades,
Your form, whose womb a fluid forearm drapes,
Is awake. Your form's awake, and your lover sees.

POEM FOUND IN *TWO YEARS BEFORE THE MAST*

Yes, whales. The first time that I heard them breathing,
We had the watch from twelve to four, and coming
Upon deck, found the little brig quite still,
Surrounded by thick fog, and the sea smooth
As though anointed with fine oil. Yet now
And then a long, low swell would rise and roll
Under the surface, slightly lifting the vessel
But without breaking the water's glassy skin.
We were surrounded far and near by shoals
Of sluggish whales and grampuses, though fog
Prevented us from seeing them rise slowly
To the surface, perhaps lying out at length,
And heaving those peculiar lazy, deep,
Long-drawn breathings, which must ever leave
An impression of supine, majestic strength.
Some of the watch were sleeping, and the others
Perfectly still, so that there could be nothing
To break the wild illusion, and I stood
Leaning over the bulwarks, listening
To the slow breathings of the mighty creatures—
Now one breaking the water just alongside,
Whose sable body I almost fancied I
Could see despite the fog; and again another,
Just audible in the distance—until the low,
Regular swell seemed like the heaving of
The ocean's mighty bosom to the sound
Of its sublime and long-drawn respirations....

HEREFORD

Heifers' doleful lowing out in the wolds.
So blithely blue a sky and clean a light.
Sweeter arguments for design than most,
They've also unearthed flashbacks of thatched eaves
Maybe one gentle rise (and another life)
Over from here, how many burnt sheep ago.
Byword in weather's local dialect,
A shower has blown up to cut the deal
For those who gambled on being here, afield
And downwind dove-gray, low-flown nimbostratus,
Natural speech a-lolloping a spray
Of welcome, your humble servant mac-less to boot.
Stranger, confess. Some deep-dug atavism
Spurred your recurrence here in parts remote.
Well, yes... And what if they should now say, "Stay"?

FÚTBOL

As if to move a flexible sphere from here
to there with unassisted head and foot
were natural and obvious. As if
a dance could always bow to resolute
constraint and never be danced the same way twice.
As if whistles and cheers, the hullabaloo
of fervent gazers were all the music needed
to keep its players' goals in tune. So that
as they weave, dodge, collide, collapse in breathless
haystacks—and rise and fall and rise again—
we're made, if not one, then at least whole.

HADRIAN

Ambition even vast finds its limit.
But love goes undefined, a threshold crossed
As often as the passage serves to deepen
Hushed petitioners who falter toward
A torch-lit audience with the oracle.

Barricades that dammed back Caledonia
And its warriors also bridled the Empire,
Rome in its silver age a hub less driven
To centrifugal expansion via paved
Routes designed to spin out cohorts of shields
By the bronze, obedient ten thousand.
Standardized blocks constructed Caesar's rough-cut
Nec plus ultra, his full stop in stone.

A calculated number of leagues south,
Great Juno drifted into indolence.
The drowsy scepter slipping from her grasp
Clattered on tile and rolled toward the feet
Of a supple Ganymede from Greece
Who decanted an unstinting Hellenism
For the imperial eagle that had taloned
Him aloft. Dawns when light spilled over
Their tousled couch and lip met softer lip,
Northern troops with matted hair and bodies
Daubed black or red or white with crisscross signs
Glared at the horizon's show of offensive
Ramparts and raised a forest of roaring spears.
Blue chieftain eyes locked on the stoop of a hawk,
Hailed it, and exulted: "Rome will fall!"

But not yet. Hadrian bowed anointed curls
To his calyx of Falernian and drank
Their future, unaware the gods predestined
An Egyptian river whose warm genius would
Enfold and waft away the drowned cupbearer,
A mutable ephebe all seven hills
And loyal provinces agreed to mourn.

Less a ruin now than breached and broken
Stonework, their eclogue is subscribed in full,
Bearded and beardless actor a dialogue
In the flickering amphitheatre
Where incident and passion, distilled as fable,
Manage not to drown in history.
They approach, take hands, embrace, and breathe a name.
When Caesar steps from loosened Tyrian robes
And youth lets fall its chlamys, not even empire
Outweighs the body's marble capital.
Cold centuries of sentries pace the wall,
Leaving it at last to midnight's legions,
The diamond surveillance of the northern stars.

LETTER TO JAMES FENTON

James, transposing the stock opening
in which letter-despatcher invites
a friend to dinner, let me begin
with thanks for lunch at Long Leys Farm—and
for coming to fetch me at the steps
of the Ashmolean in Oxford.
Details will by now have blurred a bit:
When we drove up, from your door Darryl

emerged, epitome of soft-voiced
intelligence provided with skills
to manage a buoyant reunion
after I'm guessing more than five years.
Since you had a meal to assemble,
he volunteered to pilot my tour
of the grounds, first to their wilder part,
a pond where…herons?—yes, splashed and dove.

Beyond that, an Audenesque pylon,
modernizing the rural *laisser*
aller. And here the garden proper,
room after thick-petaled, leafy room,
rain-soaked annuals, perennials,
shrubs and trees, the plant kingdom given
a path to expression fresh enough
to leave me speechless. Talk resumed, though,

when I met your gardener and saw
how diligence could implement plans
an envisioner dreams and lays out.
Double capability, meanwhile,
had called us to a light, tasty lunch.
My topic: the morning spent in Prints
and Drawings, holding pen-and-ink works
by Samuel Palmer—among them

the age-twenty self-portrait in tan
and olive wash with gesso highlights.
Was it resolve or innocence that
spurred him to ponder wells reflecting
a hurt so much in earnest? And then
disclose what surfaced, youth's native gaze
conceived as elegy; and, in that
line, not surpassed by any artist.

More than most, James, you've been the poet
as traveler, appearing in "all
the wrong places," ironic Johnny-
on-the-spot for the fall of Saigon
and more gruesome junctures in recent
South Asian history. Now, after
a century of mass murders, how
to trump burnout if those listening

are too few to reverse the onrush
of disaster? I sensed world travel
no longer drew you, that you'd come home,
content to book passage on frigates
moored in your library. Couldn't they
hoist anchor straight off for classical
sites like *Animula Vagula*,
Ut Pictura Poesis, *Cras Amet*,

and current equivalents as well?
Call for imaginative passion
and you declare for justice also.
Beginning at the breakfast table:
distinct, low-key habits of *concert*
were discernible in that duo
I overheard, its reflexive poise
a moving contrast with the single
estate, or with partners less well matched....

Funny, I don't recall our goodbyes;
which probably would have been succinct.
But pictures so clear remain, it feels
as if I never entirely left.

Bond Street Station Underground

A fly-by cinematic apparition
Where window after sliding window past

Frames a supporting cast you never saw
Before—the student's dreadlocks spilling sidewise

When he laughs and bends his bearded grin toward
The girl with green tattoos and air-blue tube top—

The older person in widowed taupe, who blinks
At the tract her silver spectacles are trained on—

The City-bound executive with shiny
Pink tie and pin stripes angled at odd vectors—

A reddish fluff of curls and rope of pearls
That somehow match the surplus weight, say, "Flo"

Put on this spring when, what, her marriage ended.
She hefts herself up doorward, steps out slowly,

Glares at your stare. Unless you fancied her?
No. Or… Fresh blossom on a Maytime bough,

Lyrics once revered that now no longer
Reread you…. You leave them untouched. So what,

Get on, get on with it. But why? Because
You can't just stand there. Far away, in close-up,

They're filming us, and other eyes are watching.

SNOW BAGATELLE

Forecasts suggest that by the end of the line
I'll think of "awkward" as… adaptable,
sort of, a playground dodge away from glibness,
in favor of, say, genitive abundance.
 "The poet," a student once wrote, "didn't mean that,
but she could of, and I prefer my interpretation."
What does any of us ever reflexively do
but botch the lyric we read up and fit it
to our own thoughts? Otherwise even
small words like *snow* would be illegible,
their definitions hard as permafrost.

Autobiographical chronicles,
the last word in affirmative disclosure,
haven't to date narrated how—and time
they did—one preschool solo rhythm section
latched onto phrases like "hickory-dickory-dock"
because their nonsense pierced him with strange relation,
which then could be made free with. It's wonderful
('smarvelous?) at that age I should of cared
to play with sounds and language, whether or not
hickory smoke or flowering trees or apples
make stronger sense impressions than words do.

The first nine chapters of *I Chronicles*
are taken up with genealogies, long lineages
put into verses without using lineation—
how a "house" continued from its genesis
through multiple generations or else
petered out and arrived at the finish line.
Spending so much time on begetting
'sprobably a waste, though the awkwardness
might remind you of a nursery rhyme, even a cursory
reading of which shows that a word like "dickory"
'sbeen jobbed in purely for its sonic impact.
Words' toylike aspect can make you bust out laughing,
though, meanwhile, no one seems to manufacture
toy fruit or flowers. You could say Beethoven,
in his *Bagatelles*, generated a whole symphony
'sworth of peak experiences, but poured into
multifaceted shot-glasses of piano music.

I think I once did (in a playhouse) drink coffee
from a toy cup—Jamaican Blue Mountain, on whose high,
cool ridges snow-white flowering trees diffused
a fragrance sword-like in its pungency.
Awkwardness, a shy glance, and a sense of play
can be a lift, a velvet revolution, along the lines
of the movement (joke) that Sworthword and Ridgecole launched,
where common speech and ballads fused into a refusal
of a batch of chronically frozen meanings that might of
fit someone else's but would close off your own thinking.
Well intentioned they no doubt were, and well designed;
but what you'll always want to bring to your own
table's the cool and awkward words you really like.

LETTER TO GRACE SCHULMAN

Dear Grace, I'm here, Lake Como has signed on
Its old adherent. How much has changed since you
Yourself pushed back this terrace chair (or one
Like it) to drink in the symphonic view?

Well, names and faces of men who wait the tables;
Mavericks among us don't wear ties at dinner;
A windstorm took out several trees last April.
But otherwise? It's just what you remember.

I've got two rooms, each with a balcony.
Of course I *could*, instead of writing, loaf,
A goldbrick working on his tan, carefree
As crowds the ferries tirelessly unload,

Who ransack portside shops for souvenirs
Or fashions. No, I'll stick to projects planned,
Sift through events that marked these past few years,
Laugh, groan, prepare for what the next will send.

At twenty-five I vowed I'd never make,
As oldsters did, docs, pills, and cures obsessive
Topics when my turn to ramble came.
Therefore no litany of crises, aggressive

Treatments, patch-ups or anesthetics. "Praise
Being," Grace, is your artist's manifesto—
Here put in handsome Lombard paraphrase
By light, lake, mountain, garden, fig, the best of

All possible perspectives. Granted, this visit
Will probably have been my last, the once
And future perfect sweetness done. But isn't
Salt always part of the taste of jubilance?

A pinch adds gusto to those melons that
Top off our dinners. Meanwhile how to praise
If we don't consume (or "vanish") each dessert—
Much as famished time soon vanishes

Us. Meals, then, are rehearsals for the last
Scene of the docudrama.... No, we're not
There yet, I do see pink and gold clouds massed
Above the peaks, as you would point them out;

Am breathing recommended redolence
Of flowerets on shrubs that scent the park,
Their Latin name, let's say, *Esthesis fragrans*,
Sensation being art's primary earmark.

So can we keep this tandem promenade
Going? Stabs in the lower lumbar region
Say no. Horace is desk-bound, I'm afraid,
And not outdoors; but soon will have permission

To stand, stretch, take a stroll down to the water.
I hope the above will bring back something of
The place you knew. If descriptions do cohere,
Credit goes to that old adhesive—Love,

CONNECTEDNESS OF ALL THINGS

The PC, on, but idle nearly an hour,
bestirred itself, volunteered a command:
and, look, a page sliding out from the printer—

blank, except for one small heart
recorded in the upper left
corner of the sheet.

*

During the July 4th concert on the town
green across the street a local band
struck up "Take the A train."

Not a week later, and pranksters have moved
one of two painted picnic tables into the
brook, where it looks like a bridge.

*

The custom, very ancient
in Middle Eastern countries,
of planting a vine at the door of a house.

*

A black leather glove weighing down,
no, shoving the handcuffed suspect's head
as he's hustled into the police car.

*

In Tenniel's *Alice* illustration
his complacent Dodo presents
the surprised heroine with a thimble.

*

Dusk fills the room where even so
you make out hands that from time
to time move pieces over the chessboard.

*

Several cities now boast residences
designated as The Poe House,
whether or not he lived in them.

*

He said, "You look at things from a
bizarre standpoint after witnessing
gunfire cut off a man at the knees."

*

X-formatted signs at train track
intersections, with RAILROAD reading down
and CROSSING aimed upward.

*

The televised statesman
bent toward a thicket of microphones,
smiled, inhaled, and said, "Friends…"

*

Lewis and Clark blazed a trail for Custer and his battle.
After which, the Sioux took paper money from soldiers' bodies
and gave it to their children, who rolled the bills into toy teepees.

*

In bas-relief profile, the Dutch cook
plays a cameo role
on a square of baker's chocolate.

*

The scene in *Scarface* when Tony's sister,
eyes overflowing, aims a pistol
but then can't bring herself to shoot him.

*

In the late 19th century men started using
initials as first names—practice
resisted by writers before A.E. Housman.

*

She said, "Any poet, year after year,
decade after decade, the subject of elegies
is clearly invincible and immortal."

Domus Cærulea

This sky afloat with cirri lacked a road map.
A Roman engineer called to survey it
Served eight summers, elated as a lover
All over again when handed new instructions.

Constructions as buoyant as desirable
Are able to hold in balance complex strains,
Extraneous yet consonant information.
Masons struck by Corona's starry chord

Record the constellation on a cork board
Covered now with green and light-blue pins.
Blueprints atop the tilted drafting table
Double the arc of love that lofted the dome,
The dominant harmonics an upraised
Appraisal of the day that lights our sky.

New England/China

Wakefield: Did some romantic alderman
Settle that name on our recycled mill-town?
I know Rhode Island is *Red* Island, or
Island of Roses... And, look, buds on Mother's
Haviland china, fifty years of attic
Storage ended, are pink, flushed with excitement
At being propped in ranks along the plate-rail
Of cabinets a shipwright made for this
Centenarian house I signed the deed on
Nine days ago. No way would I have served
Dinner on old porcelain in designer
Manhattan, my home turf for more than half
A prodigal life-span once I'd waved goodbye
To the South. But here it fits, a tasteful, gold-rimmed
Victorian replacement for the showy
Chinese export bowls and plates how many
Prosperous New England tables boasted
Back in the bullish age of clipper ships.
Those clashing pinks and reds epitomized
Spice roses of the Indies gunboats opened
To enrich our Union, sea to shining sea.

Following the *Vicar of Wakefield's* homely
Advice, I've put a "Rose Medallion" teacup
(Bought for two dollars at a thrift shop) here
In this eastern window so its damasked pattern
Can go translucent as light rejuvenates
A naïvely rendered pride of mandarins
Hard at their silken round of tea and gossip
And poetry. The Vicar's older daughter
Olivia, the more romantic one,
Might have been charmed to join their circle, even
If her graver sister, Sophia, wouldn't want to.

Goldsmith, Mother most likely never read,
But *Gone with the Wind* she surely did and like
White Southern women of her day (except
The ambitious few who idolized Miss Scarlett)
Modeled herself on Melanie—for instance,
She never told black friends and workers they
Should "know their place" and stay in it. Her son,
If he works up his nerve, can copy her
(And risk a snub) by taking lemon pie
To the family next door, whose ancestry
Is African; and probably Narragansett,
Too, or else Pequot. Out beyond the teacup
I see their children, the older climbing up
On the garbage bin while holding an umbrella,
A taut silk octagon of alternating
Ebony and ivory pie-wedge panels
That read as either a black Maltese cross
Against a cream-white background, or a white
Against a black. She's poised to make her skydive
But seems to doubt the parachute; and none
Of her younger sister's urging turns the tide.
A pause, a balance; but she doesn't leap—
The Sophia of this family circle, just
As her wilder sibling's the Olivia.
Now their mother's called them to lunch, their game
Shelved with no decisions made, no plunge
Into the aerial realm of weightless pleasure.
I'll have my solitary codfish on
These resurrected roses—a chance to ponder
The leap I leapt in settling here and calling
The Ocean State, at last, the Golden Decades'
Ultimate Cathay. So, veteran frigate,
You, unlike the *Pequod,* may now dock
And prove that not all sexagenarians
Are skippers hot to tap-dance round the deck
Like Ahab, thirst for blood a scorching trade wind
That gives them forward thrust. The middle ground!
Vicarious pastimes, watching children's games
Or tending post-colonial and post-
Postmodern gardens, should amount to a sound

Retirement plan, Sophia, calm, deific
Wisdom, serving as hand-hewn figurehead
When our vessel comes to port. If goods we heft
Down the gangplank are only earthenware,
So be it, Yankees also favor those,
Judging from shards of broken plates and cups
I dug up planting the hybrid tea a friend
Gave me, the spot selected not haphazard,
Instead, exactly where a rose should go.
He laughed when told I'd named the house Knew Place—
A tribute to comedy's most tragic playwright.

But try to name or know a place you never
Lived in: Beijing. Nablus. Kabul. Baghdad...
Imagination's olive branch stops short,
Absorbing the news that soldier and civilian
Sprawl face down in crimson pools enlarged
With all they owned, one clotting upshot of
Capitalism's abstract cannibalism.
Prosperity. Ours, but insubstantial,
Like all dream-castles based on greed, up there
Above the law. Who'd listen if I called
Our captains by their real names? They won't,
Conceded, but it doesn't seem to matter.
Out of the deeps, a voice: *Permission denied.*
No port for the tempest-tossed, you haven't yet
Begun to fight. Weigh anchor and make ready
For the clash. While you breathe, you won't retire.

ANTARCTIC

Polar, antipodean, the father King
penguin would (if penguins did) think of us
as bodies hanging downside up, footsoles
sticking to the planet's inhospitable,
broiling half.

Pinfeathers glossy-smooth as ermine, the lower
part of his dinner suit can incubate
an oval solid, resting on black talons—
one blood-warm venture left to him in trust
the morning mother brooders metronomed
off on their way to ice brinks overland.
Instinct and hunger pushed them, plunged their flock
into resounding tanks of turquoise brine
to gulp a cache of fish for transport home.

*

The orange tint suffusing his broad chest
outglows this July afternoon's decline
below horizons an ice age froze and locked
in place. To either side, cold high-rise silences
take the austral light, washes of blush rosing
a continent's sheer quartzite crags and spars
as dusk's slow indigo engulfs the valley.

He lifts and flaps his baffles
to test whiffling accelerations in the air.
Hardened, compliant, still, he'll crane his head
and look: it's bearing down, an ambush of white
artillery, whiplash bulletins forewarning
close-huddled bodies of the siege to come.

*

Birds at the margin get the brunt of it,
including one we've watched, who leans towards
the flock's pulsating hub, his back abraded
by icy needles. One who'd elbow a path
between, among, a thousand cousins
if hindered limbs could manage
an exclusion so determined,
the blast unfavorable.
He stands and stays, giving what heat he has
to his small charge, its shell as hard as marble.

*

Morning's still aftermath. Tilted dolmen
off to himself in a drift. Encased in crystal…
And she, homing in, will find that cold pillar,
not the mate who trilled a guttural
patter-song when he courted.

*

Dismal to see them down there in their blank
contra-hemisphere, small, black-and-white
emblems for team spirit, pins attached
to a globe not brooded over half enough.

No beaklet to peep and pipe for food, cushioned
body skittering across the summer ice….

*

Human nature: it likes sad narratives.
But currents charged beyond the natural
might conceivably thaw out a captive.
This antithetical perspective, bottom
to top, allows for an alternative,
the shell's reticulations opening
on limbs snug warm in down, while seed-bead eyes
appraise new sky and snow, a twin sunrise
simmering on the ice-milk breast of giants
confirmed as shelter when their call tunes up.

FATE'S SURPRISES

When they hear mortals (*Nevermore!*)
Speak fateful words, the gods turn wry.
To knock hubris back in its place
And scoff at the vow of solitude
I'd cut in stone, they sent me you,
Love, whose good looks, mind, and senses
Are summer showers that sluice away
Stoic poses and false-heroic
History, fiction, literature.

LIGHTHOUSE

Pilot at the helm of a hidden
headland it steers free
from convergence with the freighter
when fog and storm clouds gather

Sparking communiqué no full stop ends
its broadcast sung in a three-sixty sweep
the cycle burning up five solar seconds

Midnight eye that blinks away
invisibility   a high beam
revealing as it scans whatever seas
or ships return terra firma's landmark gaze

NOTES

Resources: The line quoted is taken from Herbert's "The Collar"

Oklahoma: Rev. Allen Wright, Choctaw and appointed governor of the Choctaws in the 1880s by the U.S. government, devised a name for the state known earlier as Indian Territory. What used to be called the Five Civilized Nations were the Indians who formed Western-style governments: the Cherokee, Chickasaw, Choctaw, Creek, and Seminole.

The Red River, Cimarron, Washita, and Arkansas all empty into the Mississippi.

The first name for Tulsa was Tulsey Town, after a Creek Indian settlement in Alabama called Talasi or Tullasee Town. When the Creeks migrated to the site of modern Tulsa they designated an oak on the shore of the Arkansas as a central landmark and called it the "Council Oak." It was struck by lightning in the 1970s, and a new tree has been planted in its stead. Several oil refineries stand on the north side of the Arkansas, whereas the southern side is primarily residential. "Philbrook," the Italianate Tulsa residence of oil magnate Waite Phillips, was donated to the city and houses its fine arts museum. *St. John in the Wilderness*, a painting of John the Baptist by 17th century Piedmontese painter Tanzio da Varallo, is part of the Philbrook collection. Bartlesville was the site of Oklahoma's earliest oil wells and oilmen Phillips and Getty had offices there. Also, the H.C. Price International Pipeline Company, which manufactured pipes used for the oil. In 1956 Price commissioned a building from Frank Lloyd Wright, the latter's only extant example of highrise construction. Greenwood, a neighborhood in Tulsa, where in 1921 hundreds of Black residents were killed and their houses burned during an uprising of white Tulsans. Jimmy Rushing, born in Oklahoma City, was a singer who performed with Walter Page's Blue Devils and Count Basie's band. He was called the "Oklahoma Nightingale." Ralph Ellison was born in Oklahoma City and lived in its Deep Deuce neighborhood. He studied music and was a jazz fan and expert. The Black Mesa, in the northwestern part of the state known as the Panhandle, is the highest elevation in OK.

Route 66, often driven by Jack Kerouac in the 1950s, used to run through Oklahoma City and Tulsa. Joe Brainard, a visual artist and poet, published a book titled *I Remember*, based on his memories of growing up in Tulsa. In 1970 Larry Clark published a book of photographs about Tulsa's drug subculture said to have influenced filmmakers like Martin Scorsese. Clark himself made several films, *Kids* the best known.

Oklahomans are called "Sooners" because of stories about pioneers who stole into the territory before it had been opened to settlement and staked their claims sooner than it was legal to do so. "Soonerism" is my own coinage to describe the wide variety of pithy expressions that can be heard in OK, especially in rural areas. In November 1974, Karen Silkwood, employed by Kerr-McGee, manufacturers of plutonium fuel, died in an automobile accident after having attended her union's meeting in Crescent, OK. Police investigation concluded that she had fallen asleep at the wheel, and an autopsy discovered a high level of Quaalude tranquilizer in her blood. In the weeks before her death she had been exposed to dangerous amounts of radiation and had registered a complaint that safety measures at the Kerr-McGee plant were inadequate. The site of Fort Sill in what is now Lawton, OK, was staked out on January 8, 1869 by Maj. Gen. Philip H. Sheridan who led a Campaign into Indian Territory to stop hostile tribes from raiding border settlements in Texas and Kansas. Today there is a United States Army installation outside Lawton. Tulsa is the site for large Lockheed Martin and Boeing plants. McAlester's McAlester Army Ammunition Plant produces most of the non-nuclear bombs used by the U.S. military. Jim Thorpe, of Sac and Fox descent, was a star athlete in several sports. A house in Yale, OK, where he lived in the 1920s, has been opened to the public.

The Wrestling Hall of Fame is located in Stillwater, on the campus of Oklahoma State University, which has had for decades an excellent wrestling team. Garth Brooks, the country singer, is an alumnus of OSU. The football team for OSU is called the Cowboys or more familiarly the Cowpokes; for the University of Oklahoma, Norman, the name is the "Sooners." Oklahoman Lynn Rigg's play, *Green Grow the Lilacs*, was produced by the Theater Guild in New York in 1931. In 1943, Rodgers and Hammerstein's musical *Oklahoma!*, based on the Riggs play, opened on Broadway. John Steinbeck's novel *The Grapes of Wrath* describes the migration of refugees from the 1935 "Dust Bowl" in Oklahoma to California. Tom Mix did in fact work as a bartender at a saloon in Guthrie, the state's first capital. The poet John Berryman was born in McAlester and lived in other towns in Oklahoma, including Anadarko. The latter is the location of the Indian Hall of Fame, an outdoor collection of busts of notable Native Americans opened in the early 1950s. Oklahoman Will Rogers, of Cherokee descent, gained fame as a vaudeville performer in the 20s and 30s, his motto, "I never met a man I didn't like."

Bricktown, an older sector of Oklahoma City, has recently been renovated, with new restaurants and cabarets as part of its attractions. The Utica Square Mall in Tulsa is the location for high-end clothing stores and boutiques. A national monument in Oklahoma City commemorates those who died in an attack on the Alfred P. Murrah Federal Building there, blown up in 1995 by Timothy McVeigh. In March of 2003, the U.S. invaded Iraq, its first target the southern city of Basra. Woody Guthrie, the folksinger, was born in Okemah, OK. Among his well-known songs is "Your Land and My Land," from which the citation is taken. Sequoyah, the Cherokee leader and writer, invented a syllabary for the Cherokee language.

Letter to Marilyn Hacker: The classical hexameter consists of five dactyls and one spondee, but substitute feet are permitted. Walter Benjamin (1892-1940), German-Jewish philosopher, expatriate in Paris during the Twenties and Thirties. Among his influential works is a study of the *flâneur* or "stroller" in French culture, the observer who wanders about the city and reflects on its sights. Belleville is a largely working-class district in the 10th *arrondissement* of Paris. The Canal St. Martin is an intra-city waterway in the northeastern sector of Paris, just south of Belleville. One of its banks is the Quai de Jemappes. Louis Aragon (1897-1982), novelist and poet, the author of *Le Paysan de Paris* (*The Countryman of Paris*, 1925), a non-dramatic and surrealistic presentation of enigmatic corners of the capital, that easily meets Benjamin's definition of *flâneur* literature. The Bibliothèque François Miterrand is France's National Library, relocated to its present site in the 13th *arrondissement* during the 1990s. A new *métro* (subway) line was built, beginning at the Church of the Madeleine and terminating at the Library. In Proust's novel *In Search of Lost Time*, the narrator's private revelations begin when involuntary memories are stimulated by the consumption of a *madeleine*, a small, scalloped-shaped biscuit, and a cup of linden-flower tea. Stéphane Mallarmé (1842-1898), Symbolist poet, once wrote, "The world was made to end in a book." Gertrude Stein and Alice B. Toklas were longtime American-born residents of Paris as well as the other lesbian writers whose names follow directly after theirs. Lutetia was the Roman name for the city that later became Paris.

Letter to James Fenton: In addition to numerous volumes of poetry, James Fenton is the author of a collection of travel essays, *All the Wrong Places: Adrift in the Politics of the Pacific Rim* (1984). The phrase "animula vagula" is taken from a fragment of a poem by Hadrian:

> *animula vagula blandula*
> *hospes comesque corporis*
> *quae nunc abibis in loca*
> *pallidula rigida nudula*
> *nec ut soles dabis iocos!*

("Little soul, charming little wanderer, guest and companion of my body, you who are about to set out for pale, rigid waste lands, no longer will you make jokes as you used to do.")

The phrase "ut pictura poesis," "a poem is like a picture," is taken from Horace, *Epistles*, Book II, 3, (see ll. 361-365). This letter to Pisos is often called the *Ars poetica*. "Cras amet," "may he love tomorrow," taken from the anonymous poem *Pervigilium Veneris*, (*The Vigil for Venus*, 350 C.E.) which begins, *Cras amet qui numquam amavit quique amavit cras amet:* "May he who never did love, love tomorrow, and he who did, may he also love tomorrow."

A NOTE OF THANKS

I would like to thank Marilyn Hacker, Robert Pinsky, and Grace Schulman for reading poems in this volume and offering helpful responses. Grateful acknowledgment also goes to the Rockefeller Foundation for a resident fellowship in 2003 at the Study and Conference Center at Bellagio, to the Berkshire Taconic Foundation for a residency in 2004-2005 at the Amy Clampitt House in Lenox, Massachusetts, to the Virginia Center for the Creative Arts for a residency in 2005, and the same for Ledig House, Ghent, New York, in 2009.

A.C.

ALFRED CORN has published eight previous books of poems, the most recent titled *Contradictions*. He has also published a novel, titled *Part of His Story*; two collections of essays; and *The Poem's Heartbeat*, a study of prosody. Fellowships for his poetry include the Guggenheim, the NEA, an Award in Literature from the Academy of Arts and Letters, and one from the Academy of American Poets. *Poetry* magazine awarded him the Levinson, Blumenthal, and Dillon prizes. He has taught writing at Yale, Columbia, Oklahoma State University, and UCLA. Since 2005, he has spent part of every year in the U.K., and Pentameters Theatre in London staged his play *Lowell's Bedlam* in the spring of 2011. In 2012, he was a Visiting Fellow of Clare Hall, University of Cambridge, preparing a translation of Rilke's *Duino Elegies*. His first ebook, *Transatlantic Bridge: A Concise Guide to the Differences between British and American English*, was published in 2012. When in the U.S., he lives in Hopkinton, Rhode Island.

CPSIA information can be obtained at www.ICGtesting.com
Printed in the USA
BVOW08s1051060316

439255BV00002B/82/P